MEXICO'S COPPER CANYON

Facts, Faces, Places, and a Smattering of Spanish

Text and Photos by

Richard Gordon
91 Jane Ann Way
Campbell, California 95008

Published by: Richard Gordon
91 Jane Ann Way
Campbell, CA 95008

Library of Congress Catalog Number 89-9128

International Standard Book Number 0-9622873-0-X

TABLE OF CONTENTS

PROFILE OF THE WORLD'S MOST SCENIC RAILROAD
AND THE WESTERN HEMISPHERE'S MOST EXCITING TRAIN RIDE

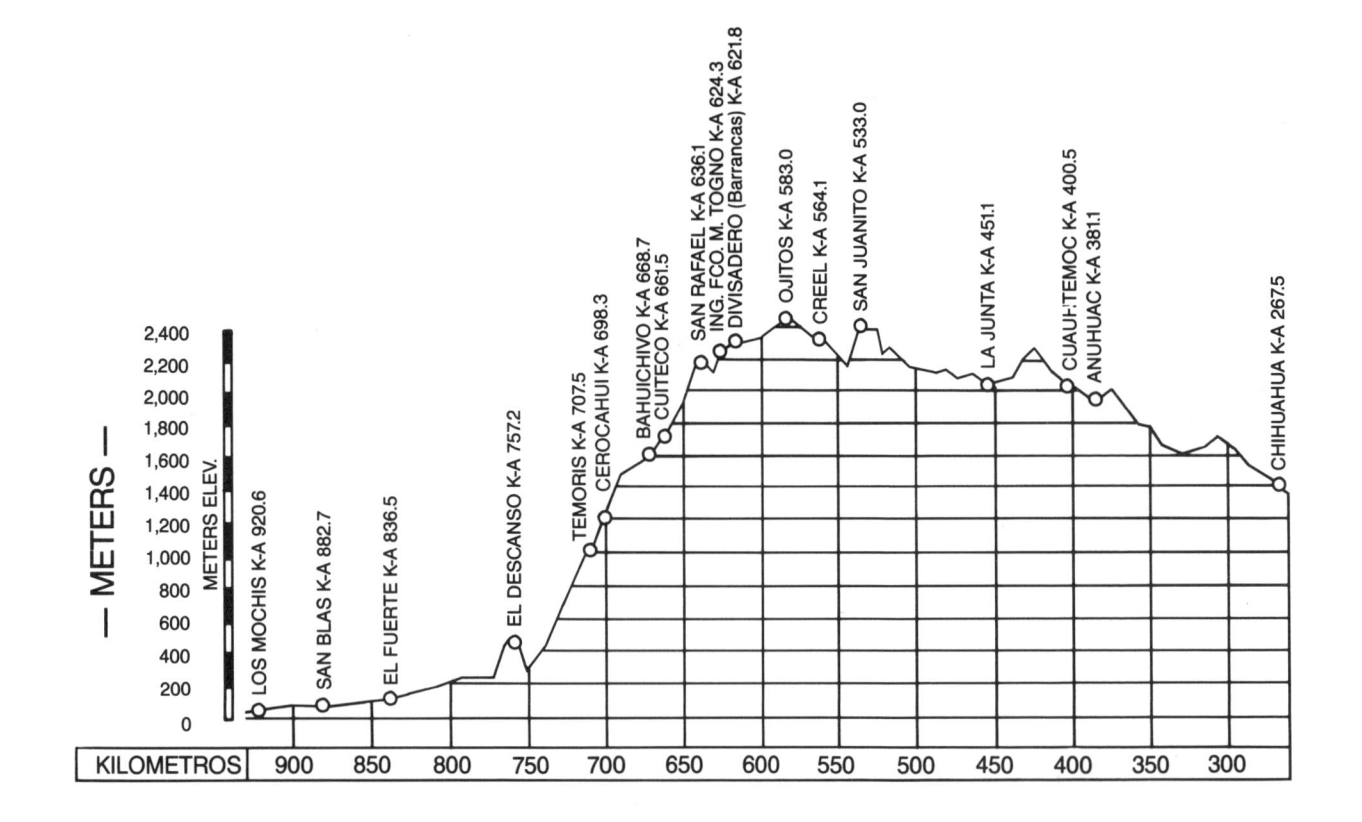

BARRANCAS AT DIVISIDERO

Why visit Mexico's Copper Canyon?

Size, for one thing. Mexicans claim that you could slip four Grand Canyons into the Copper Canyon system (which is 280 feet deeper) and have a bit of space left over.

"Just 'tain't so," say Arizonians. "Our Grand Canyon has a greater average width. Besides ours has straight up and down walls. Your canyon is V-shaped."

The argument seems certain to continue until detailed surveying of the Copper Canyon makes all the facts available. Arizonians concede, however, that the colossal Copper Canyon fissure ranks among our planet's largest.

An engineering miracle, for another. The railroad that traverses the Copper Canyon took more than $90 million and more than 90 years to build (with a revolution or two thrown in for good measure). This 406 mile long, giant roller coaster hugs precipitous hillsides, moles its way through myriad mountains, spans tiny creeks and a giant river, careens through steep canyons, doubles back on itself, and crosses the Continental divide three times.

Drama and contrast, for still another. For example, at one point (Mountain Mohinera), the canyon floor lies 12,140 feet below. Snow blankets that mountain peak in the winter, but down in the canyons oranges, bananas, papayas, and mangos flourish in a sub-tropical climate.

7

Unique Cultures. The most distinctive of which are (1) some 60,000 fair-haired, German-speaking, reserved Protestant Mennonites living in the midst of the swarthy, Spanish-speaking, outgoing Catholic Mexicans; (2) an Indian tribe whose members call themselves "the runners," who can run a deer to exhaustion; and (3) another Indian tribe that celebrates Catholic religious holidays by dancing in the streets while wearing animal masks more grotesque than those worn by our trick-or-treaters at Halloween.

Your dollar dances up and down for joy. A trip through the Copper Canyon (also known as Las Grandes Barrancas de la Tarahumara) is a dollar's delight, a place where it can do double duty. Your dollars buy the Western Hemisphere's most exciting train ride, a chance to study unique cultures, good accommodations, and all the food you can possibly eat at Mexico's bargain basement prices.

Why is this canyon called "Copper?" For one thing, its mines produced millions of dollars of copper, as well as gold and silver. For another, late in the evening, just before nightfall, the sun bathes the barrancas, warming them to a rich copper color. (If, by chance, the professional photographer's photo is a bit warmer and more "copper-toned" than yours, he's probably added a warming filter -- an 81A or 81B -- to his camera's lens.)

ONE OF MANY TUNNELS AND BRIDGES

MENNONITE CARRIAGES AT CUAUHTEMOC

Before the days of tourists and photographers -- before the days of copper, silver, and gold miners; before the days of Spanish conquerors and Catholic missionaries; even thousands of years before the days of the Tarahumara Indians, Mother Nature worked endlessly with volcanic eruptions and mighty earthquakes uplifting and upwarping the Sierra Madre into tall mountains. As she toiled, she shed a tear or two. Her tears became tiny rivulets and streams, and these in turn became the Urique, Septentrion, Batopilas, and Chinipas Rivers. Their winter torrents carved a deeper and deeper drainage system until what were once creekbeds became the majestic canyons you are about to see.

Where is (¿Dónde está?) this canyon wonderland? Look in the Northwestern corner of your map of Mexico. There you'll find the Copper Canyon (Cobre Barrancas) straddling the Mexican states of Chihuahua and Sinaloa, slicing through the heart of the Sierra Madre Occidental Mountains.

Some tourists like to start their visit in Chihuahua and terminate in Los Mochis, others prefer to do it vice-versa. What's best? A round trip. (De ida y vuelta)

Actually the biggest mistake you can make is to do this tour in a hurried, one-way, straight-through train ride of thirteen hours. If you do that, you'll miss visiting the Mennonites, the Tarahumaras, the Mayos. That's not all you'll miss. A half-dozen of the world's most colorful little villages will have slipped past your view finder. So include some stopovers -- Creel and Divisidero (or Posada Barrancas) for a minimum -- in your plan.

To get a real taste of the canyon and its cultures, take about six days with stopovers in Cuauhtemoc, Creel, Divisidero (or Posada Barrancas) and Cerocahui. The adventurous should include even a few more days for visits to the canyon bottoms, the back country, and the colorful village of Batopilas.

O.K., How? (¿Cómo?) Extremists trek in. Some even peddle their all-terrain bicycles to the rim of the canyon. Primarily though, tourists access the canyon via the train, most as regular passengers, but some with their autos strapped to flat cars, some in caravans of piggybacked RVs (recreational vehicles).

When? (¿Cuándo?) The natives say April, May, October, and November are the prettiest months. But the most exciting times, because of the Tarahumara and Mayo religious festivals, are Christmas and Easter holidays. This December/Easter peak season books early. Make your plans and reservations well in advance.

Do you speak Spanish? (Habla Usted Español?) It isn't necessary. (No es necesario). Most hotels have English-speaking personnel at the reception desk. Most restaurants and hotels provide English menus or serve family style. The bilingual host(ess) on the train calls out the towns and the interesting sights in English.

However, a few words in Spanish -- the magic words -- are fun to learn. They will smooth your way and endear you to your Mexican hosts.

Hello (Hola), Goodbye (Adiós), Yes (Sí), and No (No), If you please (Por favor)

Pardon me (Perdóneme), With your permission (Con permiso)

Thanks a lot (Muchas gracias), You're welcome (De Nada)

How are you? (Cómo está Usted?)

Fine, thanks. And you? (Muy Bien, gracias y Usted?)

Good morning (Buenos Días), Good afternoon (Buenas tardes)

Good evening (Buenas Noches)

ORIENTATION

As you travel, peer out the train window and you'll see <u>kilometer posts</u>. For example, the kilometer post at Chihuahua reads 268 km; at Los Mochis it reads 920 km. The point of reference (-- 0.0 km) is the border town of Ojinaga, situated on the Mexican side of the Rio Grande, opposite Presidio, Texas.) We'll give you the kilometer post readings for each of the best stopovers and the major points of interest. The stopover names will be in all caps. Points of interest will be in mixed capitals and small letters; both will be underlined.

<u>CHIHUAHUA</u>. (KM POST 268) -- a starting (or ending) point and a Mexican metropolis. Elevation 4692 feet; population 500,000; located 140 miles south of the border.

What does "Chihuahua" in Tarahumara mean? Take your choice. One authority says "place where sacks are made." Another says "place of two waters or a dry sandy place." A third says "place of work or place of worship." Wow, authorities can certainly be confusing!

So what does Chihuahua mean to Mexico and Mexicans? It's the capital of Mexico's largest state. It means commerce, manufacturing, and finance. It means the production of

CHIHUAHUA CATHEDRAL

cattle, alfalfa, wheat, onions, apples, timber, wood, cork, silver, lead, and zinc. To tourists: It means friendliness, hospitality, and the world's smallest dog.

Regarding these Chihuahua dogs, some say that their ancestors roamed the desert 4000 years ago. Others say the Aztecs used them for bed-warmers or occasional midnight snacks. However, a respected authority, Joaquin Ibarrola Grande, says, "This dog seems not to be from Chihuahua. It is a dog from Africa or Malta and existed in Europe centuries ago."

Actually you won't see many dogs of any variety in Chihuahua, but there are various places (because the people they honor are so significant in Mexican history) that come under the heading of "must-see." For example,

1. The dungeon of Miquel Hildalgo y Costilla (1753-1811). The people call this Catholic priest, patriot, and revolutionary "the father of Mexican Independence." The Spanish captured Hidalgo, imprisoned him in a Chihuahua dungeon, executed him, beheaded his body, and put his head on public display. (at Juarez and Guerro)

2. The statue of Benito Juarez (1806-72). A leader in the fight against the French occupation of Emperor Maximillian, Juarez inaugurated many reforms during his presidency

PANCHO VILLA STATUE

(1858-72). Should you happen to be in town on his birthday (March 21), you can see an impressive civic celebration in his honor. (at Juarez and Colon)

3. The one-time home of Francesco (Pancho) Villa (original name Doroteo Arango) (1877-1923). The home, now <u>The Museum of the Revolution</u>, exhibits many treasures from the life of a man who "wore many hats:" fugitive from justice, commander of a division of soldiers, revolutionary, jailee (suspected of treason), guerilla, governor of the State of Chihuahua, "wanted" so badly by the U.S. government that President Wilson sent troops into Mexico in a vain attempt to capture him, and hero of ballads, books, and movies. (at Calle Decima No. 3814)

Other must-sees in Chihuahua: the Cathedral (Libertad and Second) considered the state's best example of colonial architecture, the City Museum (Paseo Bolivar & Fourth), the Aqueduct (Zarco & Thirty-Second), and the University (Universidad & D. Sarmiento).

***

Now, get a good night's rest, then get up early, board the train (it departs from Chihuahua at 7 a.m., Los Mochis at 6 a.m.), and away we go! Your first (or last) point of interest:

Anahuac Station. (km post 381)   This industrial center consists of three factories: Cellulosa de Chihuahua, S.A.   produces 60,000 tons of cellulose annually; Plywood Ponderosa de Mexico, S.A., produces 2,450,000 square meters of Triplay; Viscosa de Chihuahua, S.A., annually produces 3,850,000 kilos of Texorta (an artificial fiber). These factories all use Ponderosa pine as the basic raw material.

CUAUHTEMOC. (km post 401)   Mennonite country located 65 miles (about two hours) west of Chihuahua, elevation 7200 feet, population 60,000. This is farming country, and large cylindrical grain elevators beside the train tracks provide an easy landmark.

Cuauhtemoc takes its name from Montezuma's son-in-law, the last of the Aztec emperors. Cuauhtemoc became famous for his refusal, despite Spanish tortures, to divulge the location of Montezuma's gold.

CUAUHTEMOC STATUE

MENNONITE FATHER AND SON

The Mennonites are a religious colony of about 55,000 named after the 16th-century Dutch priest Menno Simons. Most Mennonites came from Canada or Pennsylvania in 1922. At that time, Alvaro Obregon, (1880-1928) the president of Mexico, promised the Mennonites a fifty-year exemption from military service, taxation, and having to enroll their children in public schools. Mennonites preferred to establish their own schools with religion as the main course of study, instruction being given in the German language.

Originally Mennonites did not wish their children to learn any language except German, because that might cause them to become "worldly." Besides English, other worldly things to be avoided were the use of tobacco, alcohol, radios, TV, telephones, and automobiles. Lately many Mennonites have become much more permissive, speaking a bit of Spanish for business and shopping purposes. Some even speak English.

Mennonite men dress in checkered shirts, denim bib overalls, and wear straw hats. Women dress in a loose skirt and blouse, and wear a straw bonnet and scarf. If single, they wear a white scarf, if married, a black one. Mennonites tend to marry young. The average family has about ten children.

Mexicans respect their hard-working Mennonite neighbors who farm about 300,000 acres. They produce 90% of Mexico's apples and vast quantities of high quality cheddar cheese, beef, wheat, beans, and corn. They also manufacture such things as heating equip-

TARAHUMARA IN NATIVE COSTUME

ment and furniture. Visit the Mennonite cheese factory and the general store in Camp Six (about 8 miles south of Cuahtemoc).

Cuauhtemoc also makes a good starting point for a trip of six or eight hours to Basaseachic waterfall where the drop is a 1016 feet straight-down. Basaseachic means "horse's tail" in Tarahumara.

San Juanito. (km post 533) A lumber town, elevation 8000 ft.

Continental Tunnel. (km post 563) second longest tunnel on the line, 4134 feet.

CREEL. (km post 564) Pine forests, mountain meadows, curious rock formations, and Tarahumara villages surround this bustling lumber town, the center of Tarahumara country, elevation 7700 feet, population 5000, location 220 miles (about 5 1/4 hours) from Chihuahua. Hotels provide bus service from the train station. This town is also accessible from Chihuahua by auto via a newly upgraded road.

Creel takes its name from Enrique Creel, son of the American Consul. Enrique Creel became minister of foreign affairs, and a major factor in the construction of the Chihuahua-Pacifico Railroad.

VALLEY OF THE MONKS

The Tarahumaras. A unique Indian culture of approximately 60,000 members who live scattered about the hills and valleys of the Sierra Madre. Admired for keeping their culture essentially intact, these shy nomadic people are the last of the cave dwellers and the greatest of the long distance runners. They can run 500 miles in 5 days and they play 150 to 200 mile long kickball games. The kickball (about the size of a grapefruit) is carved from wood. It is kicked along (non-stop day and night) with a lifting motion of the feet. At the end of the race, the ball is the size of a golf ball.

The women's game is played with a hoop and stick. The hoop is made from thick grass or palm-like plant and the stick of pine. The stick (about a meter long) has a bent or curved end made by heating the wood. The curved end is used to lift and throw the hoop. Because of the women's many domestic duties, they only have time to run 50 miles. Tarahumaras do not schedule races and kickball competitions. Such events occur spontaneously or result from challenges and wagers.

The Tarahumaras came to the attention of the late Nathan Pritikin (founder/director of the Pritikin Longevity Center, the Pritikin Research Foundation, and author of The Pritikin Promise) at an opportune time in his life. He says, " ... at age 40 I learned I was seriously ill: I had heart disease." Thirty years later, Pritikin boasted complete recovery although he'd had no surgery, no hospitalization, and had taken no medication. How come? "I began to imitate their {The Tarahumara} dietary and exercise habits, and my

TARAHUMARA MOTHER AND CHILD

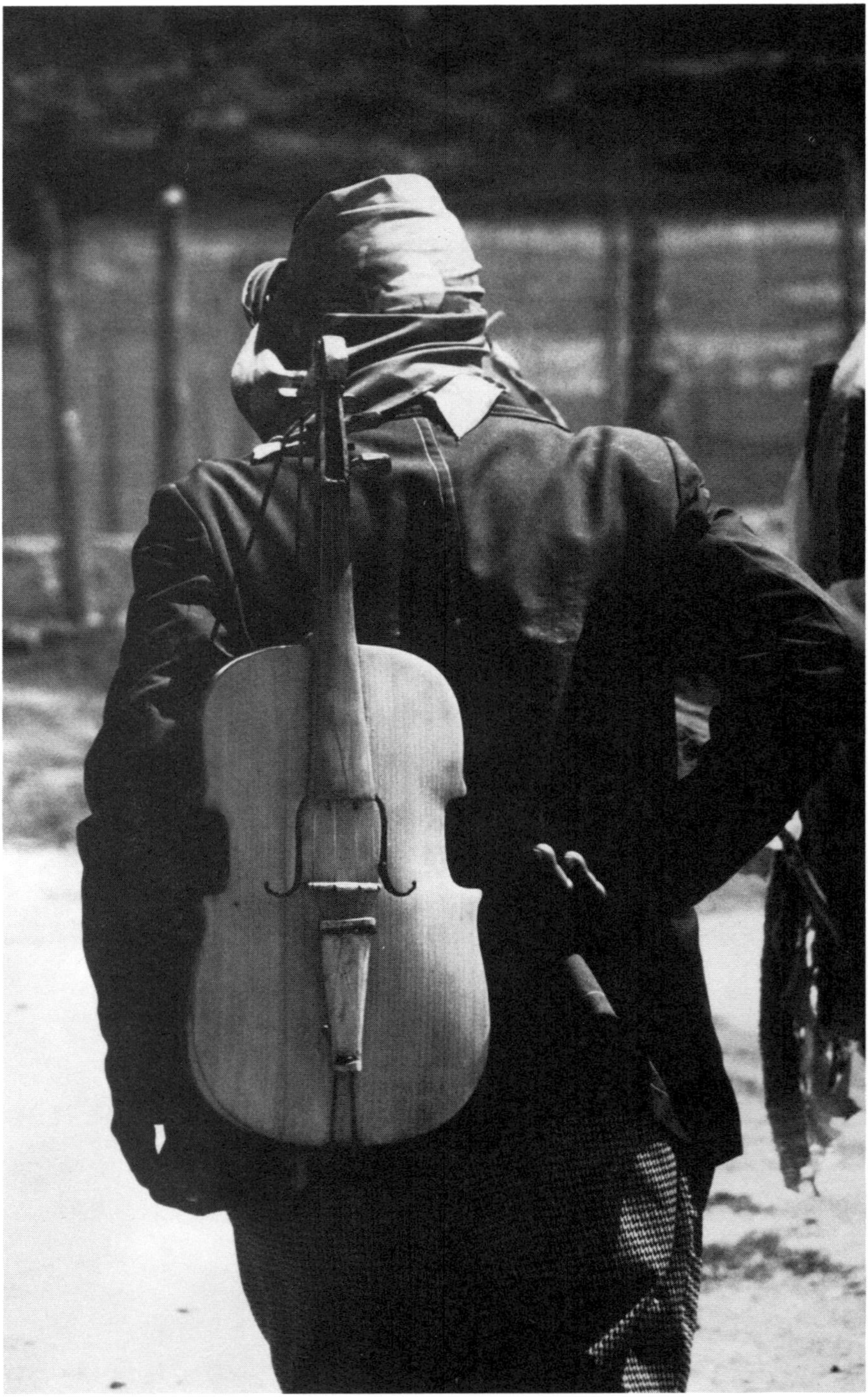

TARAHUMARA FIDDLER

recovery was underway." Their diet consists mainly of unrefined foods, corn, pinto beans, other plants, some fish, and little meat.

The religious celebrations of the Tarahumara occur on Christian holy days but blend Catholic holidays with primitive rituals. For example, in one place at the Easter Season, the Tarahumaras carve life-sized figures of Judas and his wife. After two or three days of parading them about, they tear them limb from limb and set fire to them, all to the accompaniment of incessant drumming and much tesquino (the Tarahumara homemade fermented corn drink).

The most important Catholic holy days observed by the Tarahumaras are: the 12th of December (el día de Guadalupe), Christmas (Navidad), the 6th of January (Día de Reyes) (dedicated to the three kings), and the Easter week (Semana Santa). In San Ignacio (near Creel), they also celebrate the feast of St. Ignatius (July 31).

Creel hotels offer a wide variety of tours. "Musts" include the tour to the Indian caves and a trip to the Valley of the Monks. Exciting short trips: Cusarare, the Hot Springs, the Cave Paintings, and Cusarare Waterfalls. Your most exciting short trip is to the local gift shops (best in the Northern Sierra Madre) where give-away bargains exist in

Tarahumara crafts: baskets, dolls, flutes, drums, violins, weaving, etc. (For example, a set of ten tiny nested baskets cost less than $1.50 in 1988.) Longer trips include La Bufa, Batopilas, and Basaseachic Waterfalls -- the second highest single drop in the world.

Los Ojitos. (km post 583) The highest point on the line at an elevation of 8071 feet. At such elevations bear, bighorn sheep, mountain lions, and golden eagles exist.

El Lazo. (km post 585) The railroad tracks form a complete circle here. At the point where the train tracks would close the circle, the upper part crosses a bridge while the lower part passes through a tunnel.

DIVISIDERO. (km post 622): 7800 feet elevation. Located about halfway between Chihuahua and Los Mochis, this is a 15 minute vista/photo stop at the rim of the Urique Canyon.

The Urique River (4135 feet below the Divisidero lookout) carved the Urique Canyon, part of a system collectively referred to as the Copper Canyon. Other members of the canyon system are the Batopilas, the Oteros, the Taratecua, the Sinforosa, and the Copper.

Rain or shine, Tarahumara vendors at the train stop offer dolls, beads, baskets, violins, and drums -- violins and drums in the $15 to $20 range, baskets and dolls from a

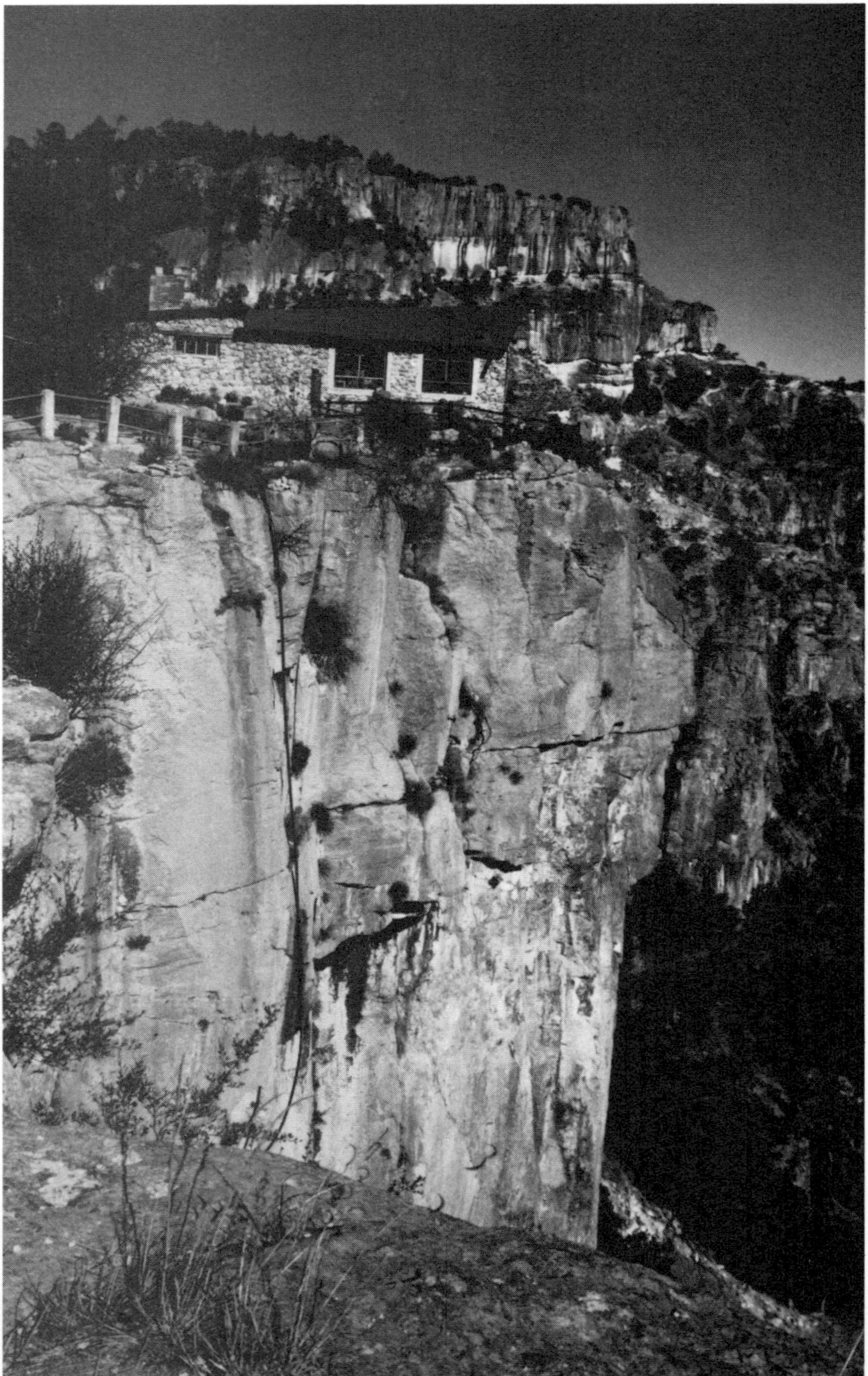

HOTEL AT DIVISIDERO

dollar up. On the hill just above the station platform you can buy tacos, burritos, and soft drinks.

Walking beyond the vendors and platform brings you to the straight-down look at the canyon and the exciting photo opportunity.

Hotel Divisidero stands at the rim of the canyon. Its comfortable rooms provide a good view. The excellent meals are served family style, and there's a reassuring fence that prevents the guests from falling to the canyon floor hundreds of feet below.

If you stay at the hotel, the walking tours to the Tarahumara caves and the tour along the canyon's rim are musts. At this elevation, in addition to the pine, you'll see madrone, manzanita, century plant, perhaps even a gray fox or an eagle.

Coping with tour guides, two-legged mountain goats with one-word vocabularies (Vámanos -- meaning let's go), poses a problem. Consequently, you'll need to learn a bit more Spanish. Two words come in very handy: "Despacio" -- (slow), and "Descanso" -- (rest).

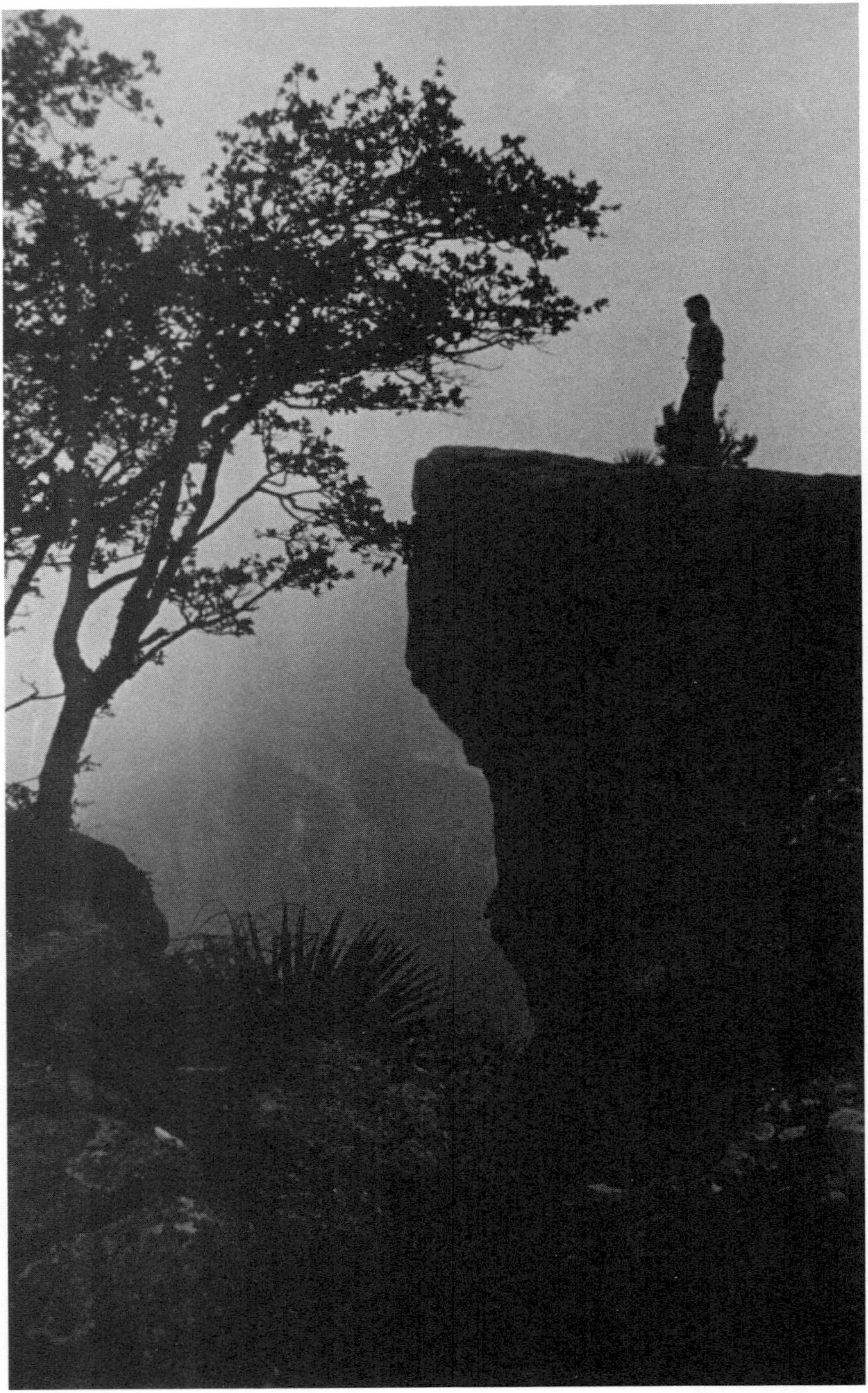

LANDSCAPE AT DIVISIDERO

TARAHUMARA CRAFTS

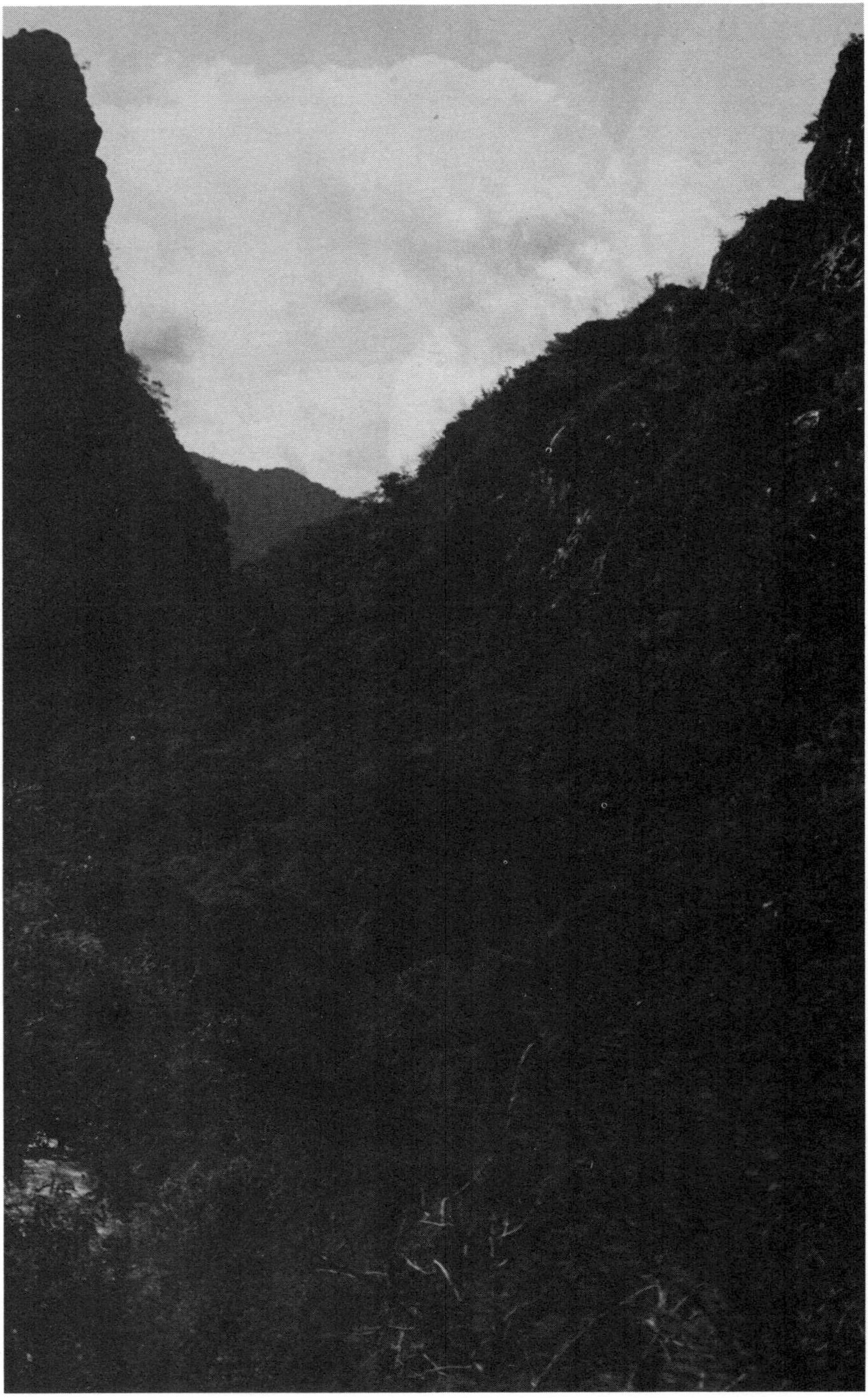

DRAMATIC LANDSCAPE

POSADA BARRANCAS. (km post 624) This hotel is located 1.8 miles south of Divisidero. ("Posada" means lodge or inn, and "Barrancas" means canyons.) The rooms, food and atmosphere are excellent. A few minutes walk brings you to a new lounge providing you one of the very best views of the canyon. Near the new lounge you'll find China Cave so called because it was once inhabited by a Chinese who worked on the construction of the railroad. Currently, a photogenic Tarahumara family inhabits the cave. Posada Barrancas' stop also serves Hotel Mansión Tarahumara.

San Rafael. (km post 636) The train stops here 15 minutes for a drink of water, a load of fuel, and a fresh crew.

CUITECO. (km post 662) A good-sized hotel with bus service and a small-sized village at 5500 feet elevation. Part of the village church is 400 years old, the other part is restored. Points of interest: the little country store, a Tarahumara boarding school, and a waterfall that the hotel brochure describes as being less than two miles away. Taking off and putting on your shoes as you crisscross the creek, the climbing under barbed wire fences, and the shortening of your breath as you clamber up steep embankments will make these two unforgettable miles the longest two miles in your life.

Bahuichivo. (km post 669) This is the train stop for CEROCAHUI, elevation 5100 feet. Catch the hotel bus to Hotel Misión (Mexicans spell "mission" with one "s.") If you

BRIDGE AT CULTECO

BURRO AT SISOGUICHIC

SCENE AT TEMORIS

ever wished to get away from it all, without giving up comfort of a good room and fine food, Cerocahui is the place you're looking for. The town is so small that streets are unnamed, the houses unnumbered.

In Tarahumara, Cerocahui means Enemy Hill, but enemies are nowhere to be seen. Instead, you'll see a golden-domed mission established in 1861 by Father Salvatierra, a Tarahumara girls' school, and the mission-style hotel.

Don't miss the bus tour to the breath-taking rim of the canyon. Take the trip to the waterfall (only a couple of hours) via horse, mule, or "shanks' mare" (your feet).

An exciting three miles with 16 tunnels. (km posts 668-707) Look for interesting landscapes and waterfalls as the train hugs the sharp hillsides of the Río Septentrión Canyon.

Temoris. (km post 708) The train crosses the Santa Barbara Bridge and stops at the station (elevation 3365 feet) for a breather. Just above the station you can see The Commemorative Plaque, a large sign with letters two feet high on rails 22 feet long built for the dedication of the completion of the line by President Lopez Mateos. You'll be able to see three levels of the railroad and waterfalls. As the train moves to the lower elevations, look

for organ pipe cactus, kapok trees, and cornfields. In winter, man-high poinsettias splotch the hillside with brilliant red.

Chinipas Bridge. (km post 748) The highest bridge on the line is 335 feet high and 955 feet long.

El Descanso (Tunnel #86). (km post 755) This is the longest tunnel (5966 feet).

The Río Fuerte Bridge. (km post 781) This is the longest bridge (1637 feet).

EL FUERTE. (km post 830) In Mayo, "the fort," was built to fend off the savage Mayo Indians. Located 50 miles east of Los Mochis at 300 feet elevation. The old buildings and cobblestone streets make this little town of particular interest.

The local hotel, Hotel Posada del Hidalgo (take hotel bus or taxi), offers lodging, meals, and fishing excursions (for large mouth bass) to the nearby Miguel Hidalgo Dam.

The savage Mayo Indians, mentioned above (now Catholics), celebrate Christmas, New Year, the Easter Season, and June 24th (the day of San Juan) wearing animal masks and shells while they dance to a drumbeat in the streets. These dances and costumes are a "must-see." The Mayos, closely related to the Tarahumaras, have become subsistence farm-

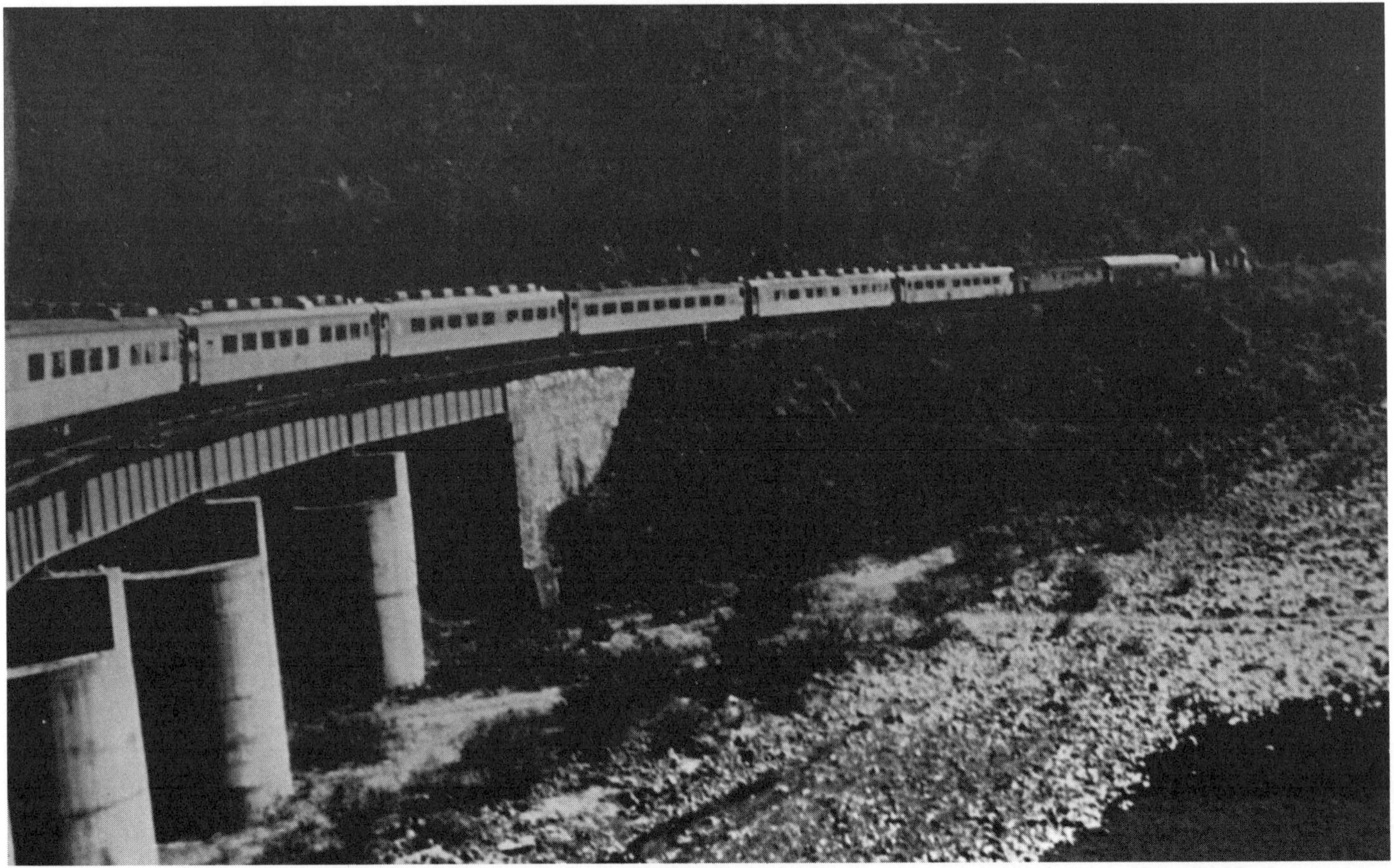

E PLURIBUS UNUM

ers, growing primarily corn, beans, squash, cotton, some cattle, and sheep. Crops are augmented by hunting and fishing. They make their houses of adobe and surround them with a yard enclosed by a woven cane fence.

San Blas. (km post 883) This is the junction (30 miles from Los Mochis) with the Pacific railroad which follows the shoreline of the Gulf of California through the states of Sonora and Sinaloa.

LOS MOCHIS. (km post 920) This modern city, elevation 117 feet, population 135,000 located 15 miles east of the Gulf of California, is the end (and/or starting) point of your tour. Take Hotel Santa Anita bus or taxi.

Los Mochis, in Mayo "place of the land turtles," was founded in 1903 by Benjamin Johnston, who saw great potential for the growing of sugar cane. Fields of sugar cane, cotton, wheat, rice, corn, flowers, and tomatoes surround the city. The biggest crop today is tomatoes.

Johnston traveled extensively and collected plants assiduously. His home, now Sinaloa Park and Botanical Gardens, exhibits many varieties of palm, shrubs, and exotic flowers. A tour of the town will take you through these gardens, through streets lined with the homes of the millionaire farmers, and to nearby Topolobampo.   Topolobampo boasts the world's third deepest harbor.

Having experienced the grandeur of the canyon; the excitement of the unique train trip; having met the Mennonites, the Tarahumaras, and the Mayos; there is yet one luxury to which you should treat yourself.

So, before you take the trip in reverse, enjoy a really fine fish dinner.   Either Los Mochis or Topolobampo makes an ideal place.

--end--

TARAHUMARA LOGO

THE CHIHUAHUA-PACIFICO RAILWAY

"The world's most scenic railroad!" "The Western Hemisphere's most exciting train ride!" "An incredible route!" How and when did it happen?

It started in 1872, in the mind's eye of dreamer, Albert Kinsey Owen, an American engineer and socialist. But the railroad was only part of his larger dream that included an Utopian socialist colony near the Bay of Topolobampo (the world's third deepest harbor) with a railroad to connect the colony to New York.

President Ulysses S. Grant expressed interest in the idea, but allocated no funds. However, in 1881, President General Manuel Gonzáles of Mexico gave Owen a concession for a transcontinental railway and a colony near Topolobampo -- the colony to be named "Gonzáles City."

No sooner were the idealistic colonists settled when Gonzáles City began to disintegrate: typhoid ran rampant. Owen failed to plan for such necessities as clean drinking water, housing, and adequate food supplies. Disillusioned, surviving members of Owen's "City of Peace" headed for home.

Surveying for the Mexican portion of the railway began in 1885. Construction started in 1898. The first tracks were laid in 1902. Construction was from the border town of Ojinaga to Creel and from Topolobampo to San Pedro. The area between Creel and San Pedro -- an area through the tortuous Sierra Madre and an area where elevation falls from about 8000 feet to 400 feet in a mere 150 miles -- had to wait.

Pancho Villa was a contractor for the building of the road in western Chihuahua. However, when the revolution came in 1912 Villa's revolutionaries constantly tore up track between Falomir, Chihuahua, and Sanchez to impede government troop movement.

Surveying of the mountainous area finally took place in 1940-2.

Eighty-six tunnels, 35 bridges, 90 years, and about 100 million dollars later, President Adolfo Lopez Mateos opened the line on November 23 of 1961.

ESTADOS UNIDOS MEXICANOS
SEC. DE GOBERNACION

PARA EL LLENADO DE ESTA FORMA UTILICE LETRA DE MOLDE.
FOR THE FILLING OF THIS FORM USE CAPITAL LETTERS.
REMPLIR CETTE FORME EN CARACTERES D'IMPRIMERE.

121 No. F ᶠᴹᵀ **3736241**

APELLIDOS SURNAMES NOMS DE FAMILLE	NOMBRE. FIRST NAME PRÉNOM.

SEXO SEX SEXE	EDAD AGE AGE	SOLTERO (A) SINGLE CELIBATAIRE 1	CASADO (A) MARRIED MARIÉ (E) 2	DIVORCIADO (A) DIVORCED DIVORCE (E) 3	VIUDO (A) WIDO W (ER) VEUF (VE) 4

0 PROFESIONAL O TECNICO PROFESSIONAL OR TECHNICIAN PROFESSIONNEL OU TECHNICIEN	1 GERENTE. ADMINISTRADOR O FUNCIONARIO DE CATEGORIA DIRECTIVA MANAGER. ADMINISTRATOR. OR ADMINISTRATIVE OFFICIAL. DIRECTEUR. ADMINISTRATEUR OU FONCTIONNAIRE ATTACHÉ DE DIRECTION.	2 EMPLEADO DE OFICINA PUBLICA O PRIVADA. EMPLOYEE OF PUBLIC OR PRIVATE OFFICE. EMPLOYÉ DE BUREAU PUBLICOU PRIVE	3 COMERCIANTE O VENDEDOR MERCHANT OR SELLER COMMERCANT OU VENDEUR
4 AGRICULTOR GANADERO PESCADOR, ETC FARMER, LIVESTOCK-RAISER FISHER, ETC. AGRICULTEUR, FERMIER. PECHEUR, ETC.	5 CONDUCTOR DE MEDIO DE TRANSPORTE. DRIVER OF VEHICLE. CHAUFFEUR DE VEHICULES DE TRANSPORT.	6 OBRERO WORKER OUVRIER	7 SERVICIOS PERSONALES PERSONAL SERVICES SERVICES DE PERSONNEL	8 MIEMBRO DE LAS FUERZAS ARMADAS MEMBERS OF ARMED FORCES MEMBERS DES FORCES ARMEES	9 ESTUDIANTE, AMA DE CASA RENTISTA, JUBILADO, MENOR STUDENT, HOUSEWIFE BOND-HOLDER, RETIRED, MINOR ETUDIANT.MAITRESSE,DEMAISON RENTIER, RETRAITE, MINEUR

LUGAR DE NACIMIENTO PLACE OF BIRTH LIEU DE NAISSANCE	NACIONALIDAD ACTUAL PRESENT NATIONALITY NATIONALITE ACTUELLE

DOMICILIO PERMANENTE PERMANENT ADDRESS DOMICILE PERMANENT

PASAPORTE PASSPORT PASSEPORT **No.**	EXPEDIDO EN ISSUED AT DELIVRÉ A

DESTINO PRINCIPAL EN LA REPUBLICA MEXICANA. MAIN DESTINATION IN THE MEXICAN REPUBLIC. DESTINATION PRINCIPALE DANS LA REPUBLIQUE MEXICAINE

MEDIO DE TRANSPORTE
MEANS OF TRANSPORTATION
MOYEN DE TRANSPORT

1   2   3   4   5   6

OTROS
OTHERS
AUTRES 7

TOURIST APPLICATION FORM

COPPER CANYON TRAVEL TIPS

ARRANGEMENTS/ACCOMMODATIONS: A wide variety of packages are available: 6, 8, and 9 day escorted tours, some of which include a side trip into the canyon via horse (caballo); backpacking tours; all-terrain bicycling tours; four-wheel-drive vehicle tours; and RV caravan tours. Elderhostel, an international program of study for the elderly, offers an onsite study class of the Copper Canyon.

If you wish to travel independently, your travel agent can customize a tour to fit your interests and needs.

BATHROOMS (baños): Where are the restrooms, please? (Dónde están los baños, por favor?) Men's is labeled "Caballeros", women's "Mujeres." Vista and Mixto train travelers will find it wise to carry toilet tissue and paper towels since washroom supplies get used up quickly.

BUSINESS CARDS: Everyone from the taxi driver on up has business cards. Be sure yours include any degrees or titles. Mexicans take degrees and titles seriously. The ultimate? Cards with photos.

COLORS:

amarillo	yellow	claro (a)	light	oscuro (a)	dark
azul	blue	gris	gray	rojo (a)	red
blanco	white	morado (a)	purple	rosado (a)	pink
cafe	brown	negro (a)	black	verde	green

CURRENT: 110 Alternating current (V ac) U.S. appliances work fine.

CUSTOMS, Mexico: (la aduana) Usually quite lenient. You may take in clothing (la ropa), luggage (el equipaje), one movie camera, one still camera (la cámara), and 12 rolls of film (el rollo). Check for more complete details.

DIFFICULTY: Moderate (no es difícil), but it's not for wheel chair travelers. On unescorted tours (and even some escorted tours), you must handle your own suitcase (la maleta). Baggage (el equipaje) is not checked through on the train, travel light.

People sensitive to altitudes of 8,000 feet may find themselves short of breath.

DIRECTIONS:

Dónde está ...?	where is ...?		
a la derecha	to the right	norte	north
a la izquierda	to the left	sur	south
todo derecha	straight ahead	este	east
a la vuelta	around the corner	oeste	west

DOCUMENTATION: (la documentación): A tourist card is required. Get one (free) at any Mexican Consulate or airline check-in counter by presenting your passport or birth certificate.

DRESS: Sport or casual. Men do not need a tie (la corbata) or jacket (la chaqueta). Even though the Catholics no longer require women to cover their heads in church, most do.

Essentials: walking shoes (los zapatos), a poncho or raincoat in rainy season, and thermals in winter.

EMERGENCY (la emergencia): If an emergency arises, go immediately to the nearest large hotel. Hotel personnel will help you find a doctor (el médico), a dentist (el dentista), or the police (la policía).

FAMILY:

madre, mama	mother	padre, papa	father
hermano (a)	brother/sister	tío (a)	uncle/aunt
esposo (a)	husband/wife	nieto (a)	grandchild
muchacho (a)	boy/girl	niño (a)	child
bebe	baby	abuelo (a)	grandparent
nieto (a)	nephew/niece	joven	youth

FILM: X-rays are hazardous to your film's health. The higher the ASA of the film and the more exposures the greater the damage. Damage is cumulative. Ask for hand inspection.

HEALTH (Salud): If you sneeze, instead of saying "Gesundheit," a Mexican will say, "Salud." You answer, "Gracias." "Salud" is also the toast when drinking.

Traveler's diarrhea (sometimes called "Montezuma's Revenge" or "The Touristas") is not generally a problem in this area. Many tourists do, however, drink only hotel or bottled water as a precaution.

Pepto-Bismol is easy to carry in chewable tablets form and may help with symptoms.

HOLIDAYS: (partial list)

1/1	Año Nuevo -- New Year's day. Midnight supper.
1/6	Día de los Santos Reyes -- day of the three kings. Gifts exchanged as at Christmas.
1/17	Día de San Antonio -- St. Anthony's day. Animals are decorated with flowers and ribbons and taken to the church to be blessed.
2/5	Día de la Constitución -- constitution day celebrates the 1857 and 1917 constitutions that govern Mexico.
3/21	Cumpleaños de Juarez -- birthday of Benito Juarez.
Hly. Wk.	Semana Santa -- the week before Easter.
Hly. Sat.	Judas' Day -- burning of figures representing Judas.
5/1	Día del Trabajo -- labor day. Parades, civic exercises, dances.
5/5	Cinco de Mayo -- celebrates the Mexican victory over the French. Fireworks, dances, parades.
5/10	Día de la Madre -- mother's day.
6/24	Día de San Juan Bautista -- Mayo Indians celebrate the patron saint in El Fuerte.
7/31	Día de San Ignacio -- Tarahumara Indians celebrate the patron saint in San Ignacio.

9/16	Día de la Independencia -- Independence day.
10/12	Día de la Raza -- celebrates Colombus' discovery of America.
11/2 to	Día de los Muertos -- day of the dead. Religious festivals with visits the cemeteries.
11/20	Día de la Revolución -- celebrates the revolution of 1910. Parades, dances, games.
12/12	Día de la Virgin de Guadalupe -- honors the Virgin of Guadalupe.
12/25	Navidad -- Christmas. Plays and religious ceremonies.
12/28	Día de Los Inocentes -- day of the innocent. The Mexican version of April fool's day.

HOTELS (los hoteles): Listed under "H" in Mexican telephone directories. In addition to lodging, meals, etc., they offer a variety of tours.

The elevator label for the street level floor (el piso) is "P.B. -- Planta Baja." Above the Planta Baja comes the 1st floor (our 2nd), then the 2nd floor (our 3rd,) etc.

"C" on the water faucet stands for "Caliente" -- hot. "F" stands for "Frío" -- cold.

LANGUAGE: The most confusing thing about the Spanish language is the custom of assigning masculine or feminine genders to all nouns. Everything is a "he" or a "she." "It" has yet to be invented.

Whereas in English we have only one definite article -- "the," in Spanish there are four: el/la for masculine and feminine singular, and los/las for masculine and feminine plural.

"The train" (a "he") is el tren. "Trains" is los trenes. "The exit" (a "she") is la salida. "Exits" is las salidas.

Just try to keep in mind that our language seems equally illogical to the Spanish-speaking. If their system begins to give you a headache, just relax. You can do this trip with a "sí" (yes), a "no (no), and a "gracias" (thanks).

LIFE IN THE MEXICAN MODE:

Breakfast (el desayuno) usually	8:00-10:00 a.m.
Lunch (el almuerzo) "	1:00-2:00 p.m.
Siesta (la siesta "	2:00-4:00 p.m.
Main Meal (la comida) "	3:00-5:00 p.m.
Dinner (la cena) "	9:00-11:00 p.m.
Discos (las discotecas) (peak)	Midnight-2:00 a.m.

Banks (los bancos) Mon. - Fri.   9:00 a.m.-1:30 p.m.
Shops (las tiendas) many stay open until 7:00 or 8:00 p.m.

LIGHT TRAVEL: Camera, reading material, and one carry-on only. Pack a change of shoes (los zapatos), extra trousers (los pantalones) (men), extra slacks (women), 2 shirts (las camisas) or blouses (las blusas), 2 changes of underwear (las ropas interior), 2 pr. socks (los calcetines), jacket (la chaqueta) with pockets, a Swiss Army knife (el cuchillo), poncho (in rainy season), razor (navaja de afeitar), toothbrush (cepillo de dientes), medication (la medicina), etc., several plastic bags, a small container of laundry soap (el jabón) and a sink plug (the universal type) so you can wash your clothes, a penlight, film, passport (el pasaporte), traveler's checks (los cheques), and your airplane tickets (los boletos de avión). In winter, take your thermals.

MAKING FRIENDS AND ACQUAINTANCES: The Mexicans are friendly and outgoing. Traveling by train will net you at least a couple of penpals and several invitations to visit: "Mi casa es su casa" (my house is your house). Of course, you are more likely to meet and mix with the Mexicans in the Vista train than in the more expensive Copper Canyon express cars.

MONEY: the peso. Bills are 500, 1000, 2000, 5000, 10,000 and 20,000. Coins are 1, 4, 10, 20, 50, 100, 200. The exchange rates vary by the day and according to where you cash your traveler's check.

Banks (los bancos) give the best rates, (only Chihuahua, Creel, El Fuerte, and Los Mochis have banks). Currency exchanges (los cambios) the next best rate. Hotels (los hoteles) and shops (las tiendas) give the lowest. Charge cards are honored only at the larger hotels and stores in the cities with banks.

The American dollar is accepted in most places. However, get some pesos (for the taxi, tips, etc.), before entering Mexico. This sign ($ -- with only one vertical line means pesos. The same sign with two vertical lines means dollars.

MOSQUITOS: Repellent may come in handy at rainy seasons.

NUMBERS: 0 cero, 1 uno, 2 dos, 3 tres, 4 cuatro, 5 cinco, 6 seis, 7 siete, 8 ocho, 9 nueve, 10 diez, 11 once, 12 doce, 13 trece, 14 catorce, 15 quince, 16 dieciseis, 17 diecisiete, 18 dieciocho, 19, diecinueve, 20 veinte, 21 veintiuno, 22 veintidos, 30 treinta, 40 cuarenta, 50 cincuenta, 60 sesenta, 70 setenta, 80 ochenta, 90 noventa, 100 ciento, 200 doscientos, 500 quinientos, 1000 mil, 2000 dos mil, 1,000,000, un millon.

NUMBERS TO KNOW: (5) 250-0123 hotline to Secretaria de Turismo, 2-22-84 and 2-38-67 for The Chihuahua Railway Co., P.O. Bx 46 (Mendez and 24th Streets), Chihuahua, Chih., Mexico.

PRONUNCIATION: The stress is on the next to the last syllable unless otherwise marked. "a" as in father; "b,v" (at the beginning of a word) as in book; "b,v" as in level; "c" as in country; "c" (before e and i) as in see' "ch" as in church; "e" as in bet; "g" (beginning of word) as in go; "g" (before e and i) as h in home; "h" is silent; "j" as h in home; "ll" as y in yes; "n" (with tilde ñ) as ny in canyon; "o" as in obey; "r" is trilled; "rr" is strongly trilled; "u" as oo in moon; "z" as s in see.

QUESTION WORDS: ¿A dónde? (where to), ¿Cómo? (how), Cual (which), ¿Cuánto? (how much), ¿Cuántos? (how many), Cuando (when), ¿De quién? (whose), ¿Dónde? (where), ¿Para qué? (what for), ¿Por qué? (why), ¿Qué? (what), ¿Quién? (who).

SIGNS:

Abierto:	open	Cerrado:	closed
Alto:	stop	Despacio:	slow
Entrada:	entrance	Salida:	exit
Dirección prohibida:	no entry	Entrada prohibida:	no admittance
Peligro:	danger	Precaución:	caution
Prohibido fumar:	no smoking		

TAXES AND TIPS (los impuestos y las propinas): Sometimes included. If not, give the waiter (el mesero) 10-20% of the bill. The porter (el portero) gets 150 to 200 pesos per bag. The maid (la criada) gets 150-200 pesos per day. Taxi driver (el taxista) doesn't usually get a tip, though you may tell him to keep the change. (Be sure to agree on the fare before you start your trip!)
Airport (el aeropuerto): Departure (la salida) tax on international flights (vuelos internacionales) $10 American.
Domestic flights (vuelos nacionales): 750 pesos.

THE TRAIN (el tren): The Copper Canyon Express cars are Amtrak quality and have a bar (el bar).

The Vista Train cars are older, a medium level of service, and include a restaurant car (el coche-restaurante).

The "Mixto" (sometimes called the "chicken train") is the cheapest. It travels with the windows open and runs on a separate schedule.

Vendors board the trains and offer soft drinks, beer (las cerveza), tacos (los tacos), tortillas (las tortillas), some fruit (las frutas), etc. The tacos and tortillas sold by train vendors typically are made in home kitchens.

Instead of buying vended food, many travelers bring snacks or picnic lunches. You'll find materials in the markets (los mercados) of Chihuahua, Creel, and Los Mochis. Try Mexican fruits: mangos (mangos), papayas (papayas), bananas (plátanos, and apples (manzanas). Get some Mennonite cheese (queso Menonitas).

VENDORS HOMEWARD BOUND

WEATHER: (el tiempo) is pleasant (agradable). However, snow covers the mountain peaks in December, and May-October is the rainy season.

The average Fahrenheit (T) temperature and rainfall (R) in inches in Chihuahua (elevation 4692 ft.) is:

	Jan	Feb	Mar	Apr	May	Jun	Jly	Aug	Sep	Oct	Nov	Dec
T	49	52	59	65	74	79	77	75	72	65	56	49
R	0.1	0.2	0.3	0.3	0.4	1.0	3.1	3.7	3.7	1.4	0.3	0.8

In Creel (elevation 7700 ft.) temperature and rainfall are:

	Jan	Feb	Mar	Apr	May	Jun	Jly	Aug	Sep	Oct	Nov	Dec
T	41	41	42	50	55	63	63	61	59	54	44	39
R	1.9	.31	.59	.55	1.1	5.3	5.3	5.5	1.1	2.6	1.3	1.8

Using the corresponding figures for your area as a point of reference, you can determine what to expect.

-- Buen Viaje!--
(Have a nice trip)

HOTELS -- PARTIAL LIST

CHIHUAHUA:
*****   Hyatt Exelaris at Niños Heroes y Independencia
****   Castel Sicomoro at Blvd. Ortiz Menal 411
****   Hotel San Francisco at Victoria 409
***   Victoria,   at Juarez y Colon

CUAUHTEMOC:
***   Motel Tarahumara Inn at Av. Allende y 5a.
***   Hotel Unión at Av. Allende y 5a.

CREEL:
***   Motel Parador de La Montaña (bus provided)
**   Copper Canyon Lodge (bus provided -- about 15 miles from town). (Room price includes meals.)
*   Hotel Nuevo (bus provided)

DIVISIDERO:
***   Cabañas (the only hotel at this stop). (Room price includes meals.)

POSADA BARRANCAS:
***   Posada Barrancas de Cobre. (Room price includes meals.)
***   Hotel Mansión Tarahumara (Room price includes meals.)

CEROCAHUI/URIQUE:
***   Misión (provides a bus from the train stop at Bahuichivo). (Room price includes meals.)
**   Cabañas Urique (provides 25 mile minibus service from stop at Bauchivo to Urique). (Room price includes meals.)

CUITECO:
**   Cuiteco (provides transportation from the train stop). (Room price includes meals.)

EL FUERTE:
***   La Posada Hidalgo (provides transportation or take taxi).

LOS MOCHIS:
***   Las Colinas, Carret. Inter. KM 15
***   Santa Anita, Leyva y Hildalgo
**   Plaza Inn, Leyva y Cardenas

(***** = most expensive, * = least expensive)

A ROOM FOR THE NIGHT

Chihuahua's Victoria Hotel at last! Dirty, exhausted, and having had a misunderstanding with the taxi driver, just arriving at the hotel seemed like a major victory. It was 9:30 p.m. I needed a room for the night.

The sight of many keys dangling from their little boxes reassured me that there were still rooms to be had. The sight of the clerk? Dark-haired, diminutive, curvaceous -- she wasn't a sight; she was a vision. I knew I'd have pleasant dreams.

As I plopped down my bag, rested my camera on the counter, and asked for a room, her dark, brown eyes popped open. She hesitated and stuttered. It was, it appeared, necessary to confer with the manager. Then she returned and issued me the keys to Room 6.

Room 6 was down the elevator to the basement, across the parking lot, at the end of a row of cabins, on the very perimeter of the hotel. The room was distant, dank, and dark. I felt as if my dream girl had banished me to outer Chihuahua. Being sentenced to a night of gas fumes, motor revvings, and brake squealings was, to put it mildly, nerve-wracking.

I'd spent the day on the Chihuahua-Pacifico Railway, journeying through Mexico's spectacular Copper Canyon -- a 400-mile drama of steep hills, tall bridges, and 86 tunnels. In order to capture the countryside with my camera, I'd stood in the vestibule for most of the 13 hours. The vestibule had a half-door, which made it possible to shoot pictures without window glass in the way. The train's diner had closed early. I hadn't eaten since lunch. It was late. I was ravenous.

Dropping my things in Room 6, I headed for the restaurant. The room assignment annoyed me. "I'm not going to put up with this without a protest," I decided. So when I passed the registration desk, I said, "I sure don't like that room. Every other time I've been in this hotel, I've had a room inside. Can't you do any better?" With downcast eyes, Miss Curvaceous changed my assignment to 207.

"Here's a tip," I said to the bellboy. "While I eat, please change my luggage from Room 6 to 207."

I felt ill at ease eating with grimy hands, but hunger prevailed. The fruit salad and tortilla soup were delicious.

Finally, Room 207! At last I could wash my filthy hands. As I lathered, I looked. What I saying the mirror was frightening. There were 86 layers of soot on my face -- one for each tunnel.   Mine was the face of a miner just up from the coal pits.   Suddenly, I understood why Miss "C" had hesitated to assign me a room for the night.

---End---

A few favorite places to eat:
In Chihuahua: Breakfast at the Hyatt - Dinner at Hotel Victoria
In Cuauhtemoc: Rickeys and Hotel Union
In Creel: Motel Parador
In Los Mochis: El Farallon

MAGNET IN MEXICO

They're the greatest endurance runners in the world. Sometimes they run 200 miles non-stop or 72 hours without a break. Now, I'm not a runner. It's possible I may never even see them race, but more than once the magnetism of Tarahumara greatness has pulled me out of my well-established orbit to Creel, a little toothpick-sized lumber town in the state of Chihuahua, Mexico.

Creel, the center of Tarahumara country, is not a typical tourist town. There are no Hyatts, no black sand beaches, no palm trees, no golf courses. Monstrous lumber trucks pothole Creel's unpaved streets. The streets get dusty in the dry season. They add two inches of mud to your height in the rainy season, and they freeze slippery solid on cold winter nights. Chickens, goats, dogs, and pigs roam them freely. Windowshopping Creel's mainstreet? It can take all of an hour, if you dilly-dally.

To get to Creel, I boarded the Copper Canyon Express at Chihuahua and traveled south about six hours into the heart of Mexico's Sierra Madre Occidental. Getting off at Creel's attendantless train station, I found a bus which jounced me down main street to Motel Parador -- where I had reservations for the two days before Christmas and Christmas day.

Creel's main street features a couple of gift shops (with Tarahumara-made fiddles, drums, masks, and other craft work). One finds a combination clothing-shoe store, a dinky grocery or two, a couple of cafes, a pharmacy, a church, a school, and three hotels (total about 60 rooms) with accommodations ranging from miserable to comfortable. But the one thing that sets lumber-town Creel and its main street apart from others (in addition to the Tarahumara Indians) is fencing. Where else can one find fences made from discarded bandsaw blades instead of barbed wire?

Though I would have preferred to photograph Tarahumara races and games, I came at the Christmas holidays to photograph the Tarahumara's religious celebrations. Christmas is on the calendar. It's anticipatable, but races and running games aren't. They just happen. Usually a wager starts the ball (and I do mean ball) rolling. Someone bets someone else, then non-stop night and day, the barefoot runners soccer a wooden ball (a bit larger than a baseball) across the country until it looks like a golf ball.

Aside from their spontaneous races and running games, however, several things make these nomadic, cave dwelling, reclusive people irresistible to sociologists, journalists, and photographers. In a world where such things rarely happen, the Tarahumaras retain their culture and ethnic identity. They eat primarily corn. Their drink is fermented corn liquor. Herbs constitute their basic source of medicine. They celebrate the Christian holidays of Christmas and Easter, introduced by the Spanish, but they celebrate them strictly Tarahumara fashion.

75

Anxiety characterized my first two days in Creel. It seemed I might not see a celebration. Neither the hotel clerk, the locals I questioned, nor Mary Neveu (resident of many years who works at the Mission Gift Shop) knew of any forthcoming Tarahumara activity. But late afternoon, December 24, a driver returning from a bus tour brought word that the Indians would celebrate at San Ignacio Misión starting about 9:30 p.m.

San Ignacio Misión in San Ignacio lies about four corrugated miles of creek bed and lumber truck roads from Creel. If Creel is a tooth-pick sized town, San Ignacio is a mere splinter. It consists of a church, a school, and one visible farm house. For $6.00 each, two other adventurous souls and I hired local jack-of-all-trades, Pedro, and his pickup to "get us to the church on time." At 9:30 p.m., we sat beside it huddled together in the pickup's cab trying to keep warm. We'd brought blankets, but the cold was winning. As we waited and shivered, we pondered the sky filled with radiating stars -- radiating only as they can when you see them far out in the country and miles from the competition of electric lighting.

It was a long wait. We wondered if the ride, about like thirty minutes inside of a clothes dryer at the laundromat, had been a wild goose chase. The church looked deserted -- the only signs of life were three lonesome figures standing beside it and warming their hands at a small fire of scrap lumber.

Suddenly, the doors opened -- the unforgettably crooked doors built to close an asymmetrical arch -- opened. A soft shaft of light reached out from the church filled with participants. The Tarahumara Christmas Eve celebration was about to begin.

I was the first "gringo" to enter. About half way up one side on a bench, I found a few inches into which I could wedge. Apprehensively, I glanced at my Tarahumara neighbors. Sensing neither welcome nor hostility, I scanned the church -- a church built like a huge match box. It has a flat roof and unfinished plank floor. Four off-white walls reached up. The front wall served as an altar. On it, kerosene lamps illumined the Virgin Mary's picture and the crude cross. The rear wall with the lopsided doors served as entry. Above the ridiculous entry doors precipitously hung a choir ledge. A ledge rather than a loft, it jutted out without rail or enclosure. A ladder of limbs provided access for any man suicidally inclined or sufficiently intoxicated to climb to the 15 foot high precipice.

Kerosene lamps, at intervals of about four paces along the side walls, provide a hazy illumination. A long narrow bench hugged the left wall. On the bench sat only men and boys, with me (one of the five attending gringos) sandwiched in. At the end of the bench nearest the altar, four Tarahumara fiddlers scraped a simple tune with repetitious rhythm -- a rhythm of four eight notes and two strongly accented quarters. The tempo was moderate, the tone (because of the metal strings) twangy, the tuning (because of ill-fitted pegs) primitive.

Diagonally across the church huddled on the floor sat some fifty or sixty women and their children. From time to time I peered in disbelief. No crying, no coughing, no squirming, no applauding -- they sat stoically for more than three hours.

Only men and boys danced -- the Virgin Mary looking down on them from the altar, the women and children looking up at them from the floor. The dancers formed two lines of about 12 with empty space between them. Most danced barefoot on hardened feet with wide spread toes. Others wore sandals cut from the tread of truck tires. Thongs fastened the sandals to their feet. Bright-colored, intricately patterned triangular bandannas covered the mouths and chins of the dancers. At their waists larger triangular scarves covered their trousers. A crown adorned each head, and from each crown trailed two-inch wide streamers three or four feet in length. As the dancers moved, the fiddlers, the feet, and the gourd rattles each shook, kept the pulsating beat.

Members of the lines met in the middle, twirled around, and returned to their places. The procedure, which started at the altar end progressed toward the entry. I was reminded of the square dance but there was no caller. All evening long the feet scuffed, the fiddlers scraped. As I watched, I worried about two men -- one at the head of the line. They wore no costume, merely levis and denim jackets. Each carried a segmented leather whip about three feet long. Obviously, they'd been drinking heavily. Were they drunks, I wondered, trying to horn in on the activities?   Later, I learned that they were part of the dance.   In fact, one was the chief.

No one seemed to tire.   After each brief silence the dancing started again.   The air was filled with dust from the unfinished plank floor, the smoke of kerosene lamps, the stench of corn liquor, and the smell of sweaty dancers.

Because of my camera with its flash attached, my intentions (despite my attempts to be inconspicuous) were apparent from the moment of entry.   A Tarahumara, who spoke broken English told me I could take flash pictures if I'd make a contribution to the church. The contribution was no problem but the mood was so deeply religious that I couldn't bring myself to raise the camera and release the shutter.   The flash just didn't fit in.

"Aha," I thought, "At least I can record the music on my cassette without distracting anyone."   And sure enough none noticed its little red "in operation" light as I turned it on and later shut it off.   I could hardly wait to get back to my hotel room and play my "treasure of the Sierra Madre."

However trying to record in the dark, I'd accidentally moved forward the pause button. I had no recording.   Imagine my disappointment and frustration.   I had no documentation of this event which had been the purpose of my trip.   Not a frame of film!   Not an inch of tape!   How could it happen to me?   79

After wasting Christmas morning, some of my self-pity dissipated. When I'd finished lunch, I recovered enough to hunt for photos. Walking to the north end of town I found nothing. I turned around and walked south. Suddenly, I stood at the intersection of Creel's main street and the road to San Ignacio. I walked toward San Ignacio as far as the cemetery. Some photographers can find interesting images in cemeteries. A few of the graves had inscribed headstones. Some had wooden markers. Some graves were mere mounds of dirt with two sticks for a cross. Many had wreaths or flowers -- but I had no appetite for cemetery photography on Christmas day.

I looked down the road to San Ignacio. Without a guide, a companion, or a bit of Spanish, I didn't have the courage to go by myself. Dejectedly, I started back for town. As I did, I spotted a fence made of used bandsaw blades instead of barbed wire. I framed a photo and released the shutter. Then adjusting my lens for macro, I moved in, knelt, and braced myself for an extreme close-up.

"Do you mind if I ask what you are doing," a voice behind me asked.

"I'm trying to photograph this bandsaw-blade fence. It's something I've never seen before," I answered turning around.

"I've never seen one before either. I'm Martin -- teach a travel class at University of Texas," said the lanky, whiskered speaker. "I missed the celebration last night, but I hear they're still dancing in San Ignacio and I'm going out there."

"Mind if I join you?"

The time passed quickly as we hiked along getting acquainted.

The Indians had moved from the church across a large corn patch to the hillside by the farmhouse. Near vertical cliffs formed a backdrop. Still in costume, the fiddles sawing, the Tarahumaras were dancing as if they had never stopped. The orchestra had been reduced from four fiddles to two, but two white plastic five gallon paint cans filled with corn liquor had been added. A cross made from two sticks stood behind the cans. From time to time, adults -- including the women -- filled half gourds from the cans and drank. The three bodies lying to one side were not corpses, it turned out, merely victims of the corn liquor. They looked like puppets laid aside by a puppeteer.

I spotted the chief. Still in levis, denim jacket and carrying his three foot segmented whip, he seemed an approachable man. "La noche. Magnífico!" I said, grabbing his hand. (He seemed to understand that I'd attended the Christmas Eve dance and was impressed.) "Magnífico," I repeated as I pressed a couple of dollars into his palm. "Photos, por favor. Photos?"

"Sí, sí," he responded. Then tucking his second, third, and fourth fingers into the palm of his hand, he extended his pinky, tilted his head back, and stuck his thumb to his mouth. I recognized the invitation as an insistence that I drink with him. In my very best non-verbal communication, I charaded inability to hold my liquor. I explained that it gave me a headache, that I didn't want join the trio of relaxed ones lying so oblivious to the beautiful weather and the important occasion. Fortunately, he understood and appeared un-offended.

The two fiddlers tuned and started their dirge again. Checking to make sure the pause button was not on, I put the cassette beside them and got some good tape. The day was sunny, the costumes brilliant, the dancers ignored me, so I got a couple of rolls of good pictures. At the next intermission, I picked up one of the fiddles and did a couple of strains of a Bach Bouree. The chief looked up in surprise, then nodded approval.

The admiration was mutual. A great guy -- the chief. And, great people -- those Tarahumaras, strictly the superlative class. They celebrate again Easter week -- with painted bodies instead of costumes. I may never see them run, but I'm feeling the magnetism of their greatness. It's tugging at my well-established orbit, trying to pull me again to Creel -- the little toothpick-sized lumber town in the state of Chihuahua, Mexico.

---End---

THE FIDDLERS AND FIDDLES OF MEXICO'S COPPER CANYON

Sixty thousand Tarahumara Indians live in the mountains of Northwestern Mexico, the area prospected by Humphrey Bogart in The Treasure of the Sierra Madre. These Indians, the last of the cave-dwellers, are the world's greatest endurance runners. Their diet and life style provide a model for the civilized world.

Is there a common denominator between these shy, nomadic people and the violinists and fiddlers of other countries? You can bet your "G" string there is! They both love the violin.

Let me have the privilege of introducing them: first, the fiddlers. Triangular-shaped red bandannas cover their mouths. Plaid wool blankets, draped over their left shoulders, cover their bodies but leave their bow arms unencumbered. Sandals, fastened by thongs tied around their ankles and cut from the tread of truck tires, cushion their calloused feet. At celebrations, the fiddlers tuck their instruments under their chins, apply the bows, and play for hours as if in a hypnotic trance.

To meet the Tarahumara fiddlers, grab a plane out of Tijuana, and fly to Chihuahua. Then climb aboard the Chihuahua-Pacifico railroad. About five hours later, you'll find yourself in a little lumber town called Creel.

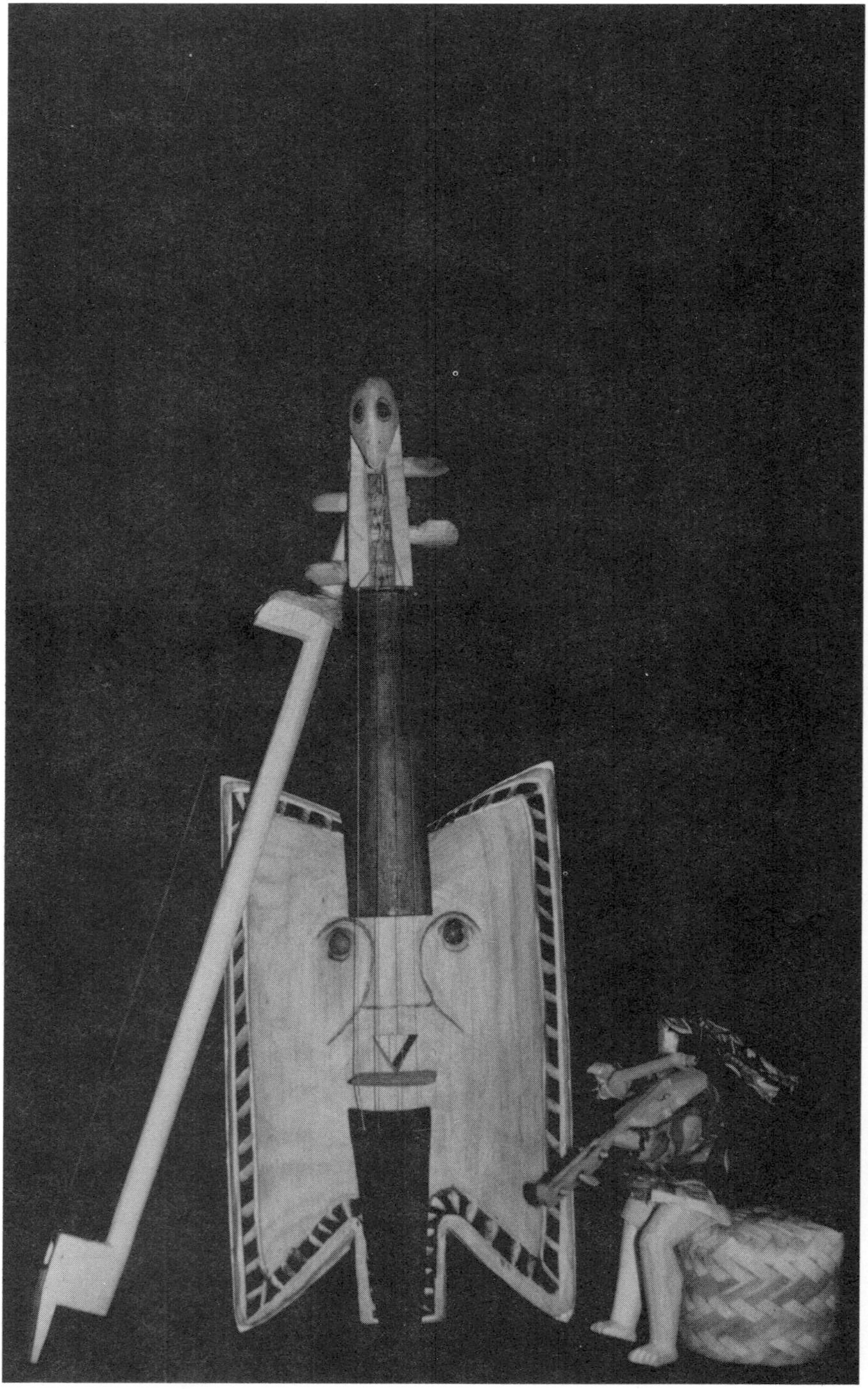

TARAHUMARA VIOLIN

Creel is the center of Tarahumara country. Dogs, goats, and pigs run loose along the unpaved main street. Several gift shops display violins, dolls, weaving, drums, and other artifacts.

Perhaps at the entrance of a shop, you'll see a woman in a dozen skirts at a time; she looks pleasingly plump. A white shawl covers her jet-black hair bringing out her skin's deep bronze tone. Like the violinists, she wears truck tire sandals. She carries a child in the blanket on her back. She has come to Creel to trade a home-made violin or, some tiny doll violinists, for skirt material. She, too, is a Tarahumara.

Steep hills of towering rock and Ponderosa Pine surround the village of Creel. In these hills -- in little cabins, and in the many caves of volcanic origin -- live the Tarahumara. Some eke out a living raising a few sheep, goats, and vegetables, or doing craft work for the tourist trade. Others migrate to lower elevations when the mud puddles in Creel's main street freeze and the snow covers the neighboring slopes.

The ruggedness of the terrain limits the deculturization which plagues so many primitive societies. That ruggedness also prevents the use of most motorized vehicles.

Getting somewhere in the Copper Canyon is a matter of walking (or running if you are a Tarahumara). The Tarahumaras call themselves, "the runners." The name fits. Any people noted for chasing deer to exhaustion, any people noted for non-stop, night and day kicking of a grapefruit-sized wooden ball across 150 to 200 miles of country, merit the name.

Such endeavors take energy. The Tarahumara eat mainly corn, beans, squash, and potatoes. Some meat is eaten, but meat eating is usually limited to ceremonial occasions. The Tarahumara lifestyle of physical activity and natural foods may well be the reason that cancer, heart-disease, and obesity are unknown to them.

These lean, hardy people were the inspiration for the work of Nathan Pritikin, founder of the Pritikin Longevity Centers. He credited them with his survival from serious heart disease, saying, "My recovery began when I began to imitate the dietary and exercise habits of the Tarahumaras." Had Pritikin played the violin, his interests would have been totally in tune with those of the Tarahumara.

Now from fiddlers, let's move to fiddles. The Spaniards came in the 17th century. Along with Catholicism, white men's diseases, horses, and cattle, they introduced the violin. Today, the violin is the Tarahumaras' favorite instrument. The violin provides the accompaniment for the religious celebrations and dances. Other instruments include the flute, guitar, and drums.

Two samples of Tarahumara philosophy reflect the place of music in their lives: "We know that when the Great Spirit created the world, He did so by singing and dancing." "Mankind devastates the face of the Earth. Because of this the Great Spirit is sometimes sad, and we must often dance the Matachin to cheer Him."

Currently, the dances and celebrations center around the Catholic holidays Día de la Virgin Guadalupe -- December 12; Navidad or Christmas -- December 25; Día de Los Santos Reyes or the day of the Three Kings -- January 6; Semana Santa or Holy Week -- Holy Thursday, Good Friday, and Holy Saturday. Although the celebrations take place on Catholic holidays, the celebrations mirror the Tarahumara traditions.

Violin making is also something the Tarahumara "do their way." Whereas our instruments tend to be standardized in body length, string length, etc., the Tarahumaras individualize each instrument. The instruments made for the tourist trade are ornate and imaginative in form. But local musicians pay more attention to playability. They use two basic types -- one shaped like well-fed violas and the other shaped like violins.

For materials, the Tarahumaras use alligator juniper, velvet ash, and a variety of cedars. The nut and fingerboard are made from denser woods, for example, the mountain

TARAHUMARA IN CHIHUAHUA

mahogany. The violins are unvarnished. Reamers being unavailable, the makers burn the pegholes. The strings are guitar strings. The poorly fitted pegs and metal strings make the instruments difficult to tune. The basic tuning is in fifths -- approximately G, D, A, E or sometimes A, D, A, E. You'll find the instruments difficult to play.

The bows tend to be heavy and convex in shape. They resemble the bows before the time of Tourte. Metal screws for adjusting bow tension are not used.

However, despite their being cumbersome, you'll admire the variety and imagination that went into the construction of these bows and instruments. Some violins have animal shapes for scrolls. Many have tops that resemble human faces.

How do such instruments sound? Beauty is in the ear of the listener it seems. Bernard L. Fontana (obviously not a member of the American String Teacher's Association), in his Tarahumara: Where Night Is The Day Of The Moon, (p. 112) says, " ... one instrument sounds like a string ensemble; with a dozen of them inside the nave of a church they produce as much sound as the whole string section of a major symphony orchestra." However, musician tourists tend to describe the sound as similar to baroque rather than symphonic.

Imagine yourself sitting on a bench in a little kerosene-lighted, plank-floored, pewless church. At the end of your bench sit four or more fiddlers. About two dozen men and boys form two lines at the altar end of the church. They wear crown-like headgear from which flow streamers.

Triangular bandannas cover their mouths, and larger triangular shapes of cloth are worn at the waist. The women and babies huddle on the floor in one corner. The men and boys proceed with the dance. The rhythms are strong, repetitious, and endless. The odors of kerosene lamp and tesqino (corn liquor) fill the air.

Despite the smells and the primitive conditions, you'll find yourself caught up in a deeply religious experience. The music fits the occasion perfectly. Of course, if you record the fiddlers and listen later (with the music out of context) you'll find the sound a bit gruesome.

Not so gruesome, however, as Traven's <u>Treasure Of The Sierra Madre</u> story, in which prospector Bogart and his companion lose their lives in search of Copper Canyon gold. Had they gone in search of something even more priceless (health, for example) they would have found it -- and a whole flock of fiddlers and fiddles besides.

-- The End --

WHY I LOVE MEXICO

(The following essay won the author a free trip to Mexico in MEXICO MAGAZINE'S Why-I-Love-Mexico contest.)

Because, when I was a stranger in their paradise, the Mexicans took me by the hand.

Traveling alone, I arrived in Chihuahua the day before Christmas. I shouldered my cameras and took to the streets to get some pictures. A trim, pleasant woman followed by two skinny boys and a big, tall husband, approached me.

"You're American, no? You are traveling alone, no?"

"Yes to both," I answered.

After a bit more conversation, she continued, "We are having our Christmas Eve celebration tonight. We'd be so honored if you would be our guest."

Somewhat later, a college-age girl approached and talked with me. "Is there some part of Chihuahua you didn't get a chance to see?" She inquired.

"I haven't yet seen the university." 93

"Here comes the bus," she said. "Let's go." I had a personally guided tour of the campus.

The little restaurant in Creel intrigued me. Once inside, I saw a young couple who had just sat down. I sensed that they might speak a bit of English.

"May I join you?" I asked.

"Please do," they said. They helped me decipher the menu and order my meal. The conversation and meal were delightful. When I got up to go, I found that my dinner was already paid for.

Sooner or later, each time I made new Mexican friends, I'd hear the phrase, "Mi casa es su casa." The words are, "my house is your house." The phrase means "you are welcome to visit me."

Lovely people, the Mexicans! The setting for the song "Take My Hand, I'm A Stranger In Paradise," is the South Pacific. But the South Pacific natives must have borrowed the idea. I know where hospitality was invented -- Mexico!

LADIES IN THE PARK

FURTHER READING

Fontana, Bernard L., Tarahumara, Where Night is the Day of the Moon. Flagstaff, AZ, Northland Press, 1979 (Informative text with excerpts from historic church documents and beautiful photographic illustrations.)

Fontana, Bernard L., The Material World of the Tarahumara. Arizona State Museum: University of Arizona, 1979.

Good, Merle, 20 Most Asked Questions About the Amish and the Mennonites. Lancaster, PA, Good Books, 1979

Kennedy, John G. and Lopez, Raul A., Semana Santa in the Sierra Tarahumara: A Comparative Study in Three Communities. Los Angeles: The Regents of the University of California.

Mason, Herbert Molloy Jr., The Great Pursuit. New York, Random House, 1977 (10,000 American troops under General Pershing enter Mexico and attempt -- but fail -- to capture Pancho Villa.)

Norman, James, "The Tarahumaras: Mexico's Long Distance Runners." The National Geographic, May 1976, pp. 702-718.

Peterson, Jessie and Knowles, Thelma Cox, ed., Pancho Villa, Intimate Recollections By People Who Knew Him. New York, Hastings House, 1977

Pritikin, Nathan, The Pritikin Promise: 28 days to a Longer Healthier Life. New York, Simon and Schuster, 1983

Sawatzky, Harry Leonard, They Sought a Country. Berkeley, CA, University of California Press, 1971 (Details of the Mennonite move from Canada to Mexico.)

Smith, Elmer L., Meet the Mennonites. Lebanon, PA, Applied Arts Publishers, 1961 (pamphlet)

Spires, Will, "The Tarahumara: Lutherie's Time-Capsule Tribe." Frets Magazine, May 1982, pp. 34-36.

Traven, B., The Treasure Of The Sierra Madre. New York, Hill and Wang, 1967, c 1935 (Exciting fiction -- the basis for the famous movie.)

Wampler, Joseph, Mexico's "Grand Canyon." Berkeley, CA, (by the author) 1978.

About The Author

Richard Gordon is a musician and teacher turned travel writer/photographer. His B.A. is from San Francisco state University and his M.A. is from San Jose State University.

He belongs to the California Writer's Club, the National Press Photographers, the Santa Clara Camera Club and he is a life member of the Musicians Union and the American String Teacher's Association.

He has contributed to MODERN PHOTOGRAPHY, THE INSTRUCTOR, MEXICO MAGAZINE, THE SAN JOSE MERCURY NEWS, THE ROSICRUCIAN DIGEST, WESTWAYS, THE TOASTMASTER, THE STRAD, THE INSTRUMENTALIST, THE MUSIC JOURNAL, etc.

His slide/tape presentations cover the Copper Canyon, Bicycling in China, Guilin -- China's Scenic City, the Great Wall of China, Hong Kong, The Valley of Kathmandu, Death Valley, and Point Lobos. About these presentations, Mr. Joe Carleton of the Sierra Club says, "These were the finest, most inspiring slide shows I've ever seen."

NEW FRIENDS (MI CASA ES SU CASA)

Riding the Chihuahua-Pacifico and visiting the Copper Canyons' little villages you're bound to make new friends. Mexicans are prone to say, "Mi casa es su casa" which means, "my house is your house" -- or please come and visit.

Name	Address	Phone

GIFT COPIES

Additional copies of this book are available postpaid for $7.95 each from the author.

Richard Gordon
91 Jane Ann Way
Campbell, CA 95008

Find enclosed check or money order for $_____

Please send _____ copies of Guide to Mexico's Copper Canyon

Name (s)_____

Address _____

City/Zip _____

(Discount available in quantities of 25 and 100)